5.00

SHELBY STEPHENSON was born June 14, 1938, on a farm at McGee's Crossroads, Johnston County, North Carolina. He was educated at the University of North Carolina-Chapel Hill (B.A., 1960), University of Pittsburgh (M.A., 1967), and the University of Wisconsin-Madison (Ph.D., 1974). His work has been published widely in periodicals and anthologies. Presently, he is associate professor of English at Pembroke State University where he teaches literature and creative writing. He is the editor of *PEMBROKE MAGAZINE*. He lives in Southern Pines, North Carolina, with his wife and two children.

Middle Creek Poems
Shelby Stephenson

blue coot press

ACKNOWLEDGMENTS

"Begging for Joy," "Daddy's Boyhood Pastime," "Gathering Scattered Corn," "Limber Neck," "When in the Sun I Dream," BACHY; "Grandpa Manly," BITS; "Hunt of Bended Knee," COLORADO QUARTERLY; "Among My Trees," "Feeding Up," INTERNATIONAL POETRY REVIEW; "Lying in the Leaves," THE LAKE SUPERIOR REVIEW; "Clematis Post," "Living Off the Land," THE LYRICIST; "Birthplace," MOUNTAIN PATHS (Anthology, SMALL FARM PRESS); "My Recurring Dream," NITTY GRITTY; "Portraits," THE NORTH CAROLINA LEADER; "When January Is Cold," OUTERBRIDGE; "To Be Borne," THE PANHANDLER; "By Uncle Reuben's Lane," "Called Country Preacher," PEMBROKE MAGAZINE; "The Graveyard Gardener," "The Old House's Brick-Oven Chimney," THE PILOT: SOUTHERN ACCENT; "Beyond a Line," ST. ANDREWS REVIEW; "Co-Cola and Hard Tack," "Tart's Fishing Worms Sold Behind the Grocery," THE SPOON RIVER QUARTERLY; "Creekwalk," STONEY LONESOME

© 1979 Shelby Stephenson
ISBN 0-932662-29-3

The Blue Coot Press
(Adjunct to St. Andrews Press)
St. Andrews Presbyterian College
Laurinburg, N. C. 28352

For Nin

CONTENTS

1

Creekwalk 10
From the Creekbed 11
Tart's Fishing Worms Sold Behind the Grocery 12
To Be Borne 13

2

Beyond a Line 16
All the Dead Goats 17
Limber Neck 18
Lying in the Leaves 19
Daddy's Boyhood Pastime 20
Hunt of Bended Knee 21

3

Begging for Joy 24
Co-Cola and Hard Tack 25
By Uncle Reuben's Lane 26
Gathering Scattered Corn 27
Feeding Up 28
When January is Cold 29

4

When in the Sun I Dream 32
Among My Trees 33
Birthplace 34
The Old House's Brick Oven Chimney 35
Portraits 36
My Recurring Dream 38
Clematis Post 39
Living Off the Land 40
Called Country Preacher 41
Grandpa Manly 42
The Graveyard Gardener 43

1

Creekwalk

Your eyes float out of sycamores,
come to me on leaves
while your hair still flows
in the limp cling of breath
and I go with poles to the water,
the lines catching bushes on the way,
footsteps left in air.
Your glances consume.

I am a rocking life.
Before my eyes a slow reed waves,
squeezing the light from my face.
I am the roam
after the horse has been stabled,
the stir pulsing away when there is no fire.
I want a heart's spring, a warm, slow heaven of stars
flowing through my veins.
I want a wind lightly
touching the small of my back.

From The Creekbed

Dark green shadows flit between leaves.
I feel rain coming and there are no drops.
Black water swirls walnuts tandem
down creek where the stump sticks out,
dead heart, leafless, no sap charging once wild veins.

Limber pole, worm in the crack in the upsidedown limb
stuffed like broccoli in the stream, smells of running bream.
Eyes turn the color of pumpkinseed, follow secret courses
where colors fade into sunfish eyes, wavering.

I need a dark leap, strike, distant run,
broke line in a wondrous path of leaving.
In my boots I sweat a realm of urgency.
When will scales scatter this ease,
spirit the rippling shoot of fin and hands?

Tart's Fishing Worms Sold Behind The Grocery

I told Lettie
we was just raising worms for Weaver,
she and the younguns counting them things—
why, it was a full-time job
and I bought them little boxes with the fishes on the sides,
ten cents a piece I paid
and I told Lettie
oyster boxes would do just as good—
paid a dollar for that whole case over there
next to that gas pump.
Weaver didn't like that, wanted that fish picture on every box—
and we was selling them to him for sixty-five cents a box
and he was selling them to the poor fishermen for $1.50.
We was busy counting worms for Weaver.
Then they got small and he said
why you're selling all your breeders
so I cut down from all these beds,
just got one now, sell worms to my friends,
must be 300 here for a dollar—
I just scoop'm in
and it don't dawn on me no more
that I'm just working for Weaver
and his big sporting goods store.

To Be Borne

Leaves loosen in late snow.
I smell the faint scent of bass bedding
under rocks, see the fanned-out holes.
Lightly, I keep eyes on the water, float
in ringed ripples with leaf-boats downcreek,
my ears lapping wooded cliffs.

2

Beyond A Line

Quiet lies the body under the limb.
Everything bends.
The pecan swells the hull.
The sun cracks sticks underfoot.
The ground's a harp strung with shadows.

Woods, I widen your tracts everywhere,
Hero of pungent trees and trickles.
I hold you in my skin, and breathe,
Rub the fresh fall of spirit all over my body,
Swim the winding tree-cliffs
With raccoons rolling in limbs.
A body rises in my mind.
Sockeyes move away from fur.

Should a jay break a day?
Feathers swim the wind in woods.
Cattle hoofs jar the earth.
Where is their dust?
In the breath blowing a ten-o'clock,
The traces taut to the plow,
All a whisper, whisper.

All The Dead Goats

Eyes light with blind poke-scrape
of barbed wire in a pasture
where dead goats lie, necks strung
on a twisted fence,
beards in the grandfather-look,
reposed in sleep
like abandoned scrub-brushes.

They could not jump the fence
to the running branch.
Their tongues roughing the dry weedlot,
risks came easy, late,
when the owner did not come.

Bellies ballooned,
thirst drove them through the barbs,
necks caught the wirewall,
the herd, charmed.

Limber Neck

Now, a chicken will eat a dead goat—
nastiest thing in the world.

He will eat a rotten chicken—carrion—anything.

I buried an old rooster one time,
didn't put him deep enough in the ground,
hogs rooted him up.

Our chickens ate those maggots.
Next morning
everyone of our twenty-two chickens
were sitting on the roostpoles—
dead—maggots gave them the limber neck.

Old Will Booie
helped us
sheet them,
toted them off
to Beaver Dam Woods,
throwed them out.

Anything rotten will kill anything.

We stocked ourselves up again.
Lord's willing,
guess them that's got, can.

Lying In The Leaves

I am troubled
by the warm blood
first lightening the carcasses
of dead animals.
Fur and feather bend
when hand touches.
The hide stiffens
before it pulls over the eyes.
I listen to the silence.

Daddy's Boyhood Pastime

I used to go lizard hunting
on old rail fences
he said.

My grandfather would make arrows
from reeds I cut in the reedmash.
I'd drive a nail or steel spike
into the arrow's end,
sticking it with gum
I got off a pine tree.
I'd twine all that.
I'd take feathers from Dominicker chickens
and wing the arrows.
The bow I made from a scalybark hickory.

Gray lizards would run those rails and I'd hunt them.

What I call racehorses—streaked lizards—would fill the hedges,
but the cats cleaned them out of this country.

Bluetailed scorpions—cats got them too.

Hunt Of Bended Knee

In the damp morning of every hunter's walking,
leaves cling to boot-soles like gumwrappers.
The fell, shouldered,
carries the absolute order of being,
the grace of dogs moving across fields
over logs, stops where every hunted thing runs.

In a vision I keep them there
midstride in harvested corn
and call up mice
Burns and Roethke would like,
root them in air juggling their soft bodies
over spared stalks and nubbins.

I ride the currents,
the taste of hard cider
flowing through my eyes
with every attempt to step.

At the rim of my hillside
where longleaf pine
green in the sun

I walk alone where once
I hunted game in woods
thick as guilt.

3

Begging For Joy

I am not the seed I was.
I squeeze the sun from the rainbow and see sweat.
Let me lead the earth to water,
Put green in the clay,
Weep the returning ocean,
Deepen this heart.

Space, pick up your feet.
Walk outside the ring.
Look! The soil is turning, the furrows make.

Co-Cola And Hard Tack

Joe Mac Parrish moved from the country to Durham.
He came back to where he growed up, said it was good,
worth coming home just to take a dump in the cornfield,
just to hear it hit the ground, just to use a corncob again.
Said how he was going to bed—then go back to that field
the next morning to see if it was still there,
see if a dog hadn't eat it.

Lexie Rideout was standing next to a tree, listening.
When Joe Mac finished, Lexie said:
"Well, I'll tell you one thing, Joe Mac. Hit'll be there,
you can count on it. Ain't no damn dog'll touch it,
you up air in Durm eatin nothin but co-cola and hard tack.
I bet you if you shape it and put in in a rifle and shoot it,
why, you'd kill a deer three mile away."

My Uncle Reuben's Lane

On a hillside
where Uncle Reuben's Lane
runs from Sister's birthplace to Roach Branch
Skeeter and I sit on curved steel
sliding over sweet potato rows
ridged like fat dirt snakes
ready to take the poke of vines
after the click and waterburst of a million dreams.

Brother Paul jaws a Brown Williamson plug
juicy like a bead about to burst
into a joyful spurt at digging time.
My quid makes me sick, I puke,
but Skeet tongues his chew up and down
every row between cowlane and woods.

In my own rolling head the land forgets I am warped
in my metal seat, strapped by a dream already past,
seeing Brother blow a Jew's harp to the owls
roosting in sycamores on the edge of Reuben's Lane,
as we handdig yams, scraping our nails on the skins,
a song empty as a pursesnap.

Gathering Scattered Corn

Burlap inked 3-9-6,
the sound of drags, trace squeaks
in corn middles, a man in faded overalls
bend from a pointillist brush.

He picks up nubbins, underhands them into a slide,
sacrifices from the land, blues,
spirituals of Jesus crying holy
from chariots swung down in fields
where hope is a longnecked drink from a trough,
sweat pouring out like a psalm.

Feeding Up

In the hallway of the stables
I race by Gray to empty the feed in Black's trough,
all the time hearing Daddy say *watch that mule,*
she'll kick you in the navel.

I press my back against the sliding door, push rollers
along the track until they fall off in the middle.
Lifting that door, I settle the wheels gently.
Behind the cowstables, at the well, Brother waters the mules,
ten buckets full, drawing the muddy chain
moving like knifeblades in his hands.

Hogs root, eat in the upper feedlot,
the feeder-doors clapping among fireflies.
Chores done, I skip to the house in the dark, tagging
with my big toe the smoothest walnut-tree root as I go.

When January Is Cold

In this ice-edged hour, this January of hog-killings,
I see the whipped creak of trace-chains
slipping under wrinkled snouts, pigs' lashes
like drawn shade-tassels hanging from closed lids,
know the running blood, the trembling jar
of heads and ears on sleds mule-drawn to the barrel
sliced in two bubbling with scalding water
triple rainbows in the sun—
I turn from the morning, and I believe:
In the first dying made in pleasure or pain and I feel the goneness,
the sacrifices piling up in the fire
growing around the lightwood knots under the vat
and in the ice melting in dribs down hanging trees
and I long for whole days of understanding
the going-out lights, the washed-in-and-out of things
in a January coming onto an old gallows tree
when hogs are shot, cleaned and carved
and salted in a box or hung up to the ceilings
in smokehouses on nails and wires to cure,
tongues dripping a language, I hear.

4

When In The Sun I Dream

Blackbirds oar the horizon
dipping their wings over grainland
easy as a groomed crew.

On the tops of trees wind stirs.
Dry ninth-month grass abides no rain.
I gaze at dead limbs of pear where a mockingbird
turns tail to open air,
giving webbed twigs of black
a jackknife of feathers and blowing.
Spiders spin a white dream in new paint.
My roots spread a longing.
When I dream, the sun waters flowers.

Among My Trees

Trees, awake! Take me home to the place on the hill.

Oak, make bases for sockball games.
Walnut, cover the blacksmith.
Chinaberry, leave brushbroom-marks around your roots.
Pear, let me climb, shake, knock with a stick
Your hefty branches, remember preserves.
Peach, clear-seeds along dikes in the oatpatch,
Let the black mule nibble your leaves.
Pine, leave long green, fallen needles.
I will rake straw in heaps onto burlap sheets,
Shoulder to roses and boxwoods.

Birthplace

Bulged in the middle from being moved,
the old house sits with calendars dated 1952.
Oil bills for the Silent Flame
yellow on a nail behind the pantry door
and I remember the heater purring
in the kitchen to warm the card-players.
Now, poke-weeds, blackberries, magnolias
surround the house, mule-lot and caved-in well.
I walk through the three rooms,
break cow-itch vines growing into window sills,
picture Sister entertaining callers in the living room,
the fire, a blue-green conversation
breathing in empty Mason jars.

The Old House's Brick-Oven Chimney

Hair rubs on the baked brick chimney behind the planked house
and it is mine, coming into being
on the homemade sockballs we hit as kids.
Using the scooped-out grill as backstop
we slam homers a country mile, chase shadows where the ball
strikes branches falling on the mound.
A canopy of oaks keeps a dome
over our heads running the one oak, two, three trees
home to the chimney where Skeeter catches
without a mask to protect his nose
broken there when a snib gets him face-on
before blood and cowlicked hair
smear the worn brick oven in the chimney on Paul's Hill.

Portraits

1

The lightning rod man
came to see Pa.
"Well, sir, these rods draw lightning.
What you do is put them on top of your house
and they'll draw it into the ground."
"Well," Pa said, "if that's so,
I'd like one
and I'd like for you to put it
out in that field."

2

When I lived in the old house
I had some scuppernong brandy,
put it in the loft in October for Christmas.
I'd sit and stare at the hole first.
Then I'd climb up the ladder;
so I took the steps down.
My toenail prints are still on those boards
where I clawed that wall trying to get up to the jug
just to smell the stopper.

3

Pa had some bees.
Thomas was putting in cotton.
Those bees got around his hair, hung.
He brushed for 200 yards, right through the cottonpatch.

4

Grandpa had bees too,
twelve gums under some horse-apple trees.
He'd knock them off, make them swarm.
Grandpa would run in the house,
bees everywhere.
Grandma got the broom that was wrung in the woods.
She'd beat windows, curtains, Grandpa, too,
trying to hit those bees.

5

Ma gave me ten cents a broom to wring straw for brushbrooms.

My Recurring Dream

I keep having this dream
in which I am a cowpasture baseball player
who writes poems part-time.
My position is centerfield.
I can catch any ball on the fly.
(Once the ball hit me on the chest.
I still bare the threadmarks.)
And can I cover ground!—
only occasionally putting my feet in cowflop
(usually when I have a poem in my head).
In my dream all poets who write
their poems in dreams prance across my mind.
Then I see the bull in the far corner of the pasture.

The Clematis Post

A scraping gentles an air of oak and mimosa
and I hear sounds of boys playing basketball in the barnyard.
The leaning pole is all that's left.

The scrape of walnut leaves
thickens my mind.
Racing the wood, I wear the night like an owl seeking the world.
Leaves begin to swirl.
Sweet Betsys scent the hedge.

Clematis climbs the basketball post
around a nail where hunters cleaned small game
hamstrung through one hind leg, dogs yelping for the hides;
Daddy, grinning, pulling the skin over bodies,
shot-holes inflamed in tender meat,
cats, behind the hounds meowing.

Hidden in my growing a growing is.
Every spring the turning leaves
scrape from brown-dry stems the hanging scraps of winter.

Living Off the Land

It's right hard to think about it.
Seems like all my mind's on the graveyards.
Pa said, "Come to see me, I won't be here long."
I think of things I'd like to do.
Now my back muscles ache.
Left leg's shorter than the other.
Used to be a strong man—pick up 500 pounds with my back, almost.

Back when I came along, everybody used to wrestle, jump—
see who could do the most work.
Now we study money.

All the big apple orchards are gone.
Insects so bad, nobody has any fruit—
peach trees, old horse apples
that came from Civil War days.
I remember the Indian and Clear-seed peach.

Hedgerows were loaded with big goose plums.
They were strewed all around the woods.
Old folks planted them for hogs to eat.

Traps in the creek.
Fish would slide over the wooden fingers.
All that, gone.

Called Country Preacher

The preacher rushes
into his sermon, suffering

happiness in the tears
that drop
in his understanding
of our miserable lot.

He cuts the air
and draws on it
magnificent scenes
in the burst of his longlegged breath.

Women rise from birthstools
in Exodus, head his people to water.
He saws the basket
and the reeds standup magically.

Grandpa Manly

Grandpa Manly
was so bowbacked
they could hardly get him in his coffin.

The Graveyard Gardener

Lifting the sun
lightening his back
he barrows among graves
fresh dirt to fill holes
burrowed and gullied
deep toward walls
of bevelled boxes.

The day's rolling,
his pipe, hat all slant,
overall galluses wrongcrossed,
fugitive himself from some cooped house
come out to light
where the only job he asked
was what he got, here taking care.

Middle Creek Poems
was designed and printed by M. McOwen.
The poems were machine set by Bill Evans &
Co. in Century old style and printed on Ultima Ivory Laid paper. The Blue Coot Press
has published this book in an edition of 500.